14	15	16	17	18	19	20	21	22	23			
40	41	42	43	44	45	46	47	48	49		51	52
66	67	68	69	70	71	72	73	74	75	76	77	78
92	93	94	95	96	97	98	99	100	101	102	103	104
118	119	120	121	122	123	124	125	126	127	128	129	130
144	145	146	147	148	149	150	151	152	153	154	155	156
170	171	172	173	174	175	176	177	178	179	180	181	182
196	197	198	199	200	201	202	203	204	205	206	207	208
222	223	224	225	226	227	228	229	230	231	232	233	234
248	249	250	251	252	253	254	255	256	257	258	259	260
274	275	276	277	278	279	280	281	282	283	284	285	286
300	301	302	303	304	305	306	307	308	309	310	311	312
326	327	328	329	330	331	332	333	334	335	336	337	338
352	353	354	355	356	357	358	359	360	361	362	363	364

For Erin Murphy, who is infinitely
encouraging and supportive
—M. P.

To Adam, to celebrate your first
trip around the sun!
—J. C.

BEACH LANE BOOKS
An imprint of Simon & Schuster Children's Publishing Division
1230 Avenue of the Americas, New York, New York 10020
Text © 2023 by Miranda Paul
Illustration © 2023 by Julien Chung
Book design © 2023 by Simon & Schuster, Inc.
All rights reserved, including the right of reproduction in whole or in part in any form.
BEACH LANE BOOKS and colophon are trademarks of Simon & Schuster, Inc.
For information about special discounts for bulk purchases, please contact Simon & Schuster Special Sales
at 1-866-506-1949 or business@simonandschuster.com.
The Simon & Schuster Speakers Bureau can bring authors to your live event. For more information or to
book an event, contact the Simon & Schuster Speakers Bureau at 1-866-248-3049 or visit our website at
www.simonspeakers.com.
The text for this book was set in Shorei Sans.
The illustrations for this book were rendered digitally.
Manufactured in China
0523 SCP
First Edition
10 9 8 7 6 5 4 3 2 1
Library of Congress Cataloging-in-Publication Data
Names: Paul, Miranda, author. | Chung, Julien, illustrator.
Title: 365 : how to count a year / Miranda Paul ; illustrated by Julien Chung.
Other titles: Three hundred sixty five : how to count a year
Description: First edition. | New York : Beach Lane Books, [2023] | Audience: Ages 4-8 | Audience:
Grades 2-3 | Summary: "This unique take on a concept book will introduce young readers to numbers both
big and small, and give them the tools to understand all of the time that passes by in mysterious and exciting
ways each year. It takes the Earth 365 days to spin around the sun. But what does that actually look like?
Find out in this fun numerical breakdown of a whole entire wonderful year!"— Provided by publisher.
Identifiers: LCCN 2022046890 (print) | LCCN 2022046891 (ebook) | ISBN 9781665904407 (hardcover) |
ISBN 9781665904414 (ebook)
Subjects: LCSH: Calendar—Juvenile literature. | Year—Juvenile literature.
Classification: LCC CE13 .P38 2023 (print) | LCC CE13 (ebook) | DDC 529/.3—dc23/eng/20221117
LC record available at https://lccn.loc.gov/2022046890

365

MiRaNDa PauL + Julien ChUNG

HOW TO COUNT A YEAR

Beach Lane Books

New York · London · Toronto · Sydney · New Delhi

It takes the Earth 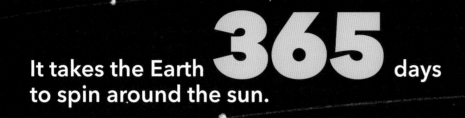 days to spin around the sun.

EARTH

That's 365 "Good mornings,"

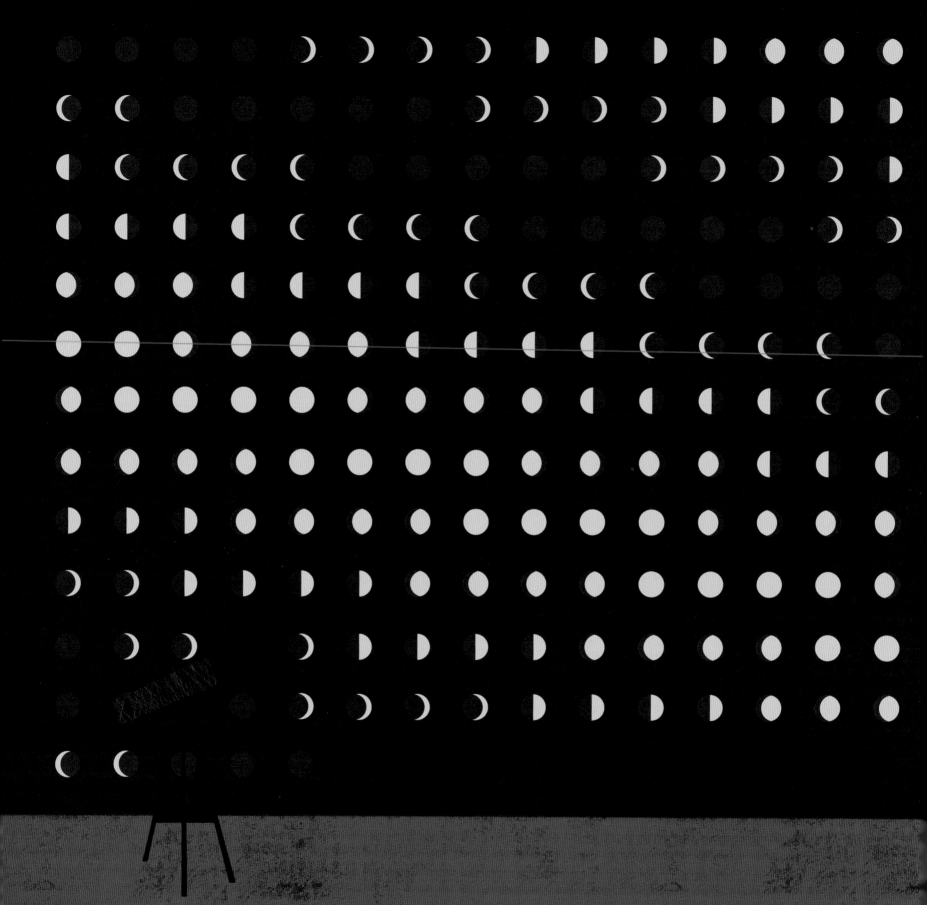

365 "Good nights,"

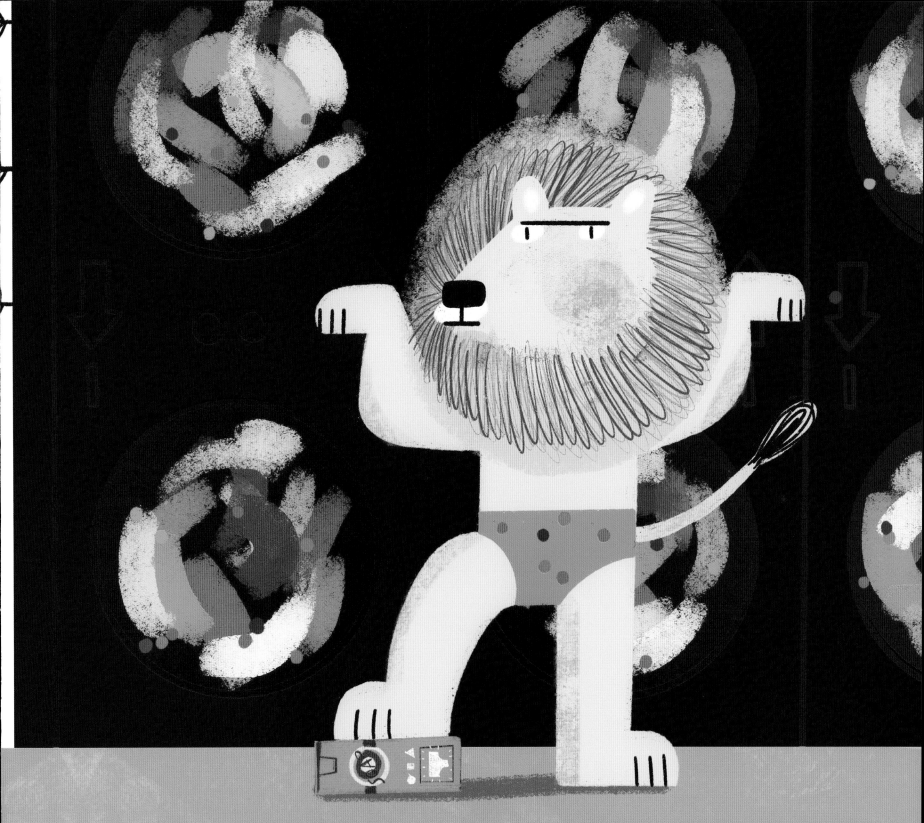

and, hopefully, 365 clean pairs of underwear.

#173   #309

sunshine scoops

One trip around the sun also means 365 flavors of the day.*

*Technically, since one year equals 365 and **one-quarter** days, every fourth year gets an extra 366th flavor. (And an extra change of undies, please!)

365 days might seem like an awful lot, so you can group the days into **52** weeks.

That could mean 52 Friday night movie popcorn spills,

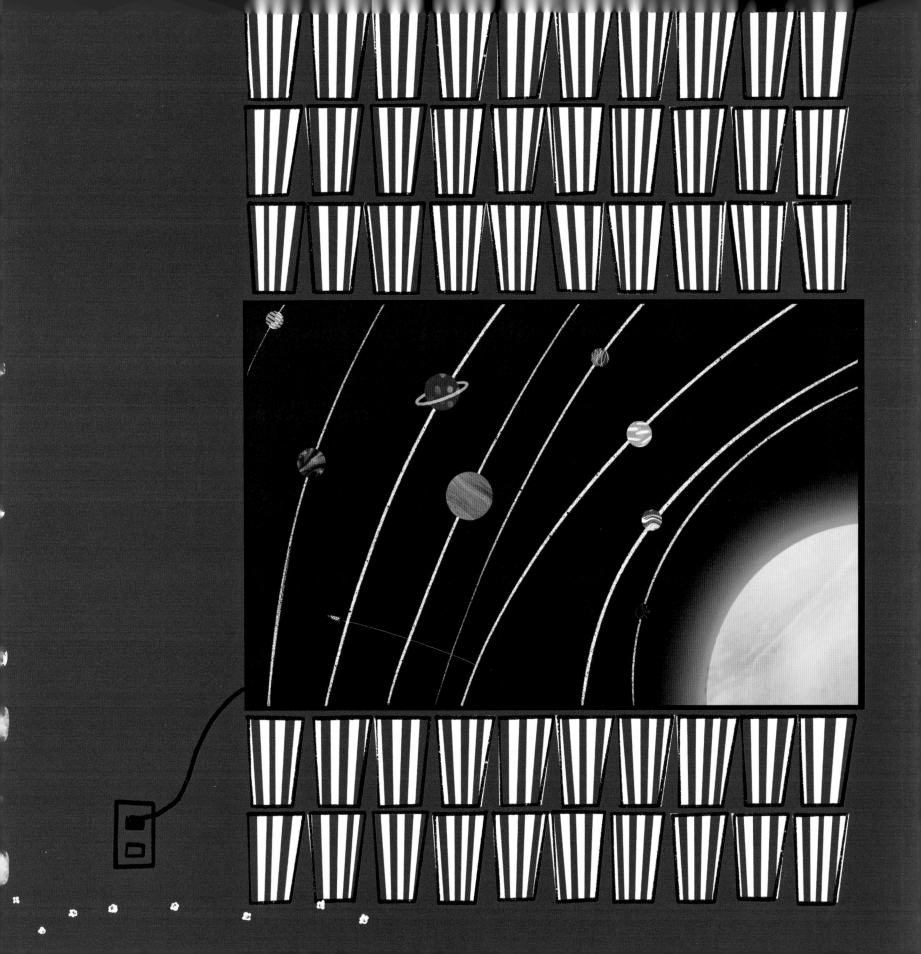

52 sleep-in Saturdays,

or 52 get-naked-and-SPLASH
Sunday baths.

Even smaller yet, 52 weeks equal calendar months.

12

That's 12 monthly clean-the-fish-tank messes,

12 bulletin-board ideas in Mr. Winner's classroom,

or 12 trips to the mailbox for
each month's magazine.

12 is an easy number to picture.

January

1	2	3	4	5	6
7	8	9	10	11	12	13
14	15	16	17	18	19	20
21	22	23	24	25	26	27
28	29	30	31			

February

				1	2	3
4	5	6	7	8	9	10
11	12	13	14	15	16	17
18	19	20	21	22	23	24
25	26	27	28			

March

				1	2	3
4	5	6	7	8	9	10
11	12	13	14	15	16	17
18	19	20	21	22	23	24
25	26	27	28	29	30	31

July

1	2	3	4	5	6	7
8	9	10	11	12	13	14
15	16	17	18	19	20	21
22	23	24	25	26	27	28
29	30	31				

August

		1	2	3	4
5	6	7	8	9	10	11
12	13	14	15	16	17	18
19	20	21	22	23	24	25
26	27	28	29	30	31	

September

						1
2	3	4	5	6	7	8
9	10	11	12	13	14	15
16	17	18	19	20	21	22
23	24	25	26	27	28	29
30						

But if we group them once more,

those 365 days
or 52 weeks
or 12 months
each add up to only . . .

April

1	2	3	4	5	6	7
8	9	10	11	12	13	14
15	16	17	18	19	20	21
22	23	24	25	26	27	28
29	30					

May

		1	2	3	4	5
6	7	8	9	10	11	12
13	14	15	16	17	18	19
20	21	22	23	24	25	26
27	28	29	30	31		

June

					1	2
3	4	5	6	7	8	9
10	11	12	13	14	15	16
17	18	19	20	21	22	23
24	25	26	27	28	29	30

October

	1	2	3	4	5	6
7	8	9	10	11	12	13
14	15	16	17	18	19	20
21	22	23	24	25	26	27
28	29	30	31			

November

				1	2	3
4	5	6	7	8	9	10
11	12	13	14	15	16	17
18	19	20	21	22	23	14
25	26	27	28	29	30	

December

						1
2	3	4	5	6	7	8
9	10	11	12	13	14	15
16	17	18	19	20	21	22
23	24	25	26	27	28	29
30	31					

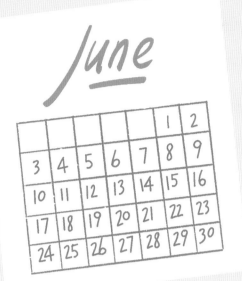

That's 1 birthday cake,
1 birthday wish,
1 birthday party
(unless you get 2!)

how long until next year's celebration?

And right after that party is over,
you'll probably start asking . . .

for 1 special YOU.

The answer—
8,760 hours—
might seem like forever.

525,600
minutes
could drag on
and on
and on
as you wait
and wait
and wait.

You might lose your cool counting

31,536,000

tick-tick-**tick-ticks** on that clock.

But the good news is that you can group those
SECONDS INTO MINU
INTO HOURS AND HOU
SUNRISES AND GOO
GOOD NIGHTS AND C
UNDERWEAR, FLA
FRIDAY NIGHT SPI
SLEEP-INS,

TES AND MINUTES
RS INTO SUNSETS AND
D MORNINGS AND
LEAN (OR DIRTY)
VORS OF THE DAY,
LLS, OR SATURDAY

so the countdown simply becomes . . .

1 marvelous collage
of 1 year
in the life
of you.

4

How will you count **your** year?

What Is a Calendar?

A calendar is a system—a specific way—in which we can count chunks of time, usually in days. If you live in the United States, you might see a calendar in your classroom that labels months and days of the week, starting with Sunday.

Many kinds of calendars are based on the sun, moon, or stars. Other calendars mark time through climate, seasons, weather, or other natural cycles. Groups of people who share a similar history, culture, tradition, or faith might use a particular calendar to mark important dates or count time in meaningful ways.

Creatively Counting Your Year

A year can take a long time to pass by. While we wait in between birthdays, there are many methods we use to measure—or put into numbers—what happens during those weeks and months. Calendars help us count, but there are other ways we can keep track of time. All our bodies are different, and people live and behave differently, but we can make some guesses—called estimates or averages—that show us how much can happen in one year.

Hair Growth: 4-6 inches

School Time: 1,260 hours

Outdoor Time: 618 hours

Full Moons: 12 or 13

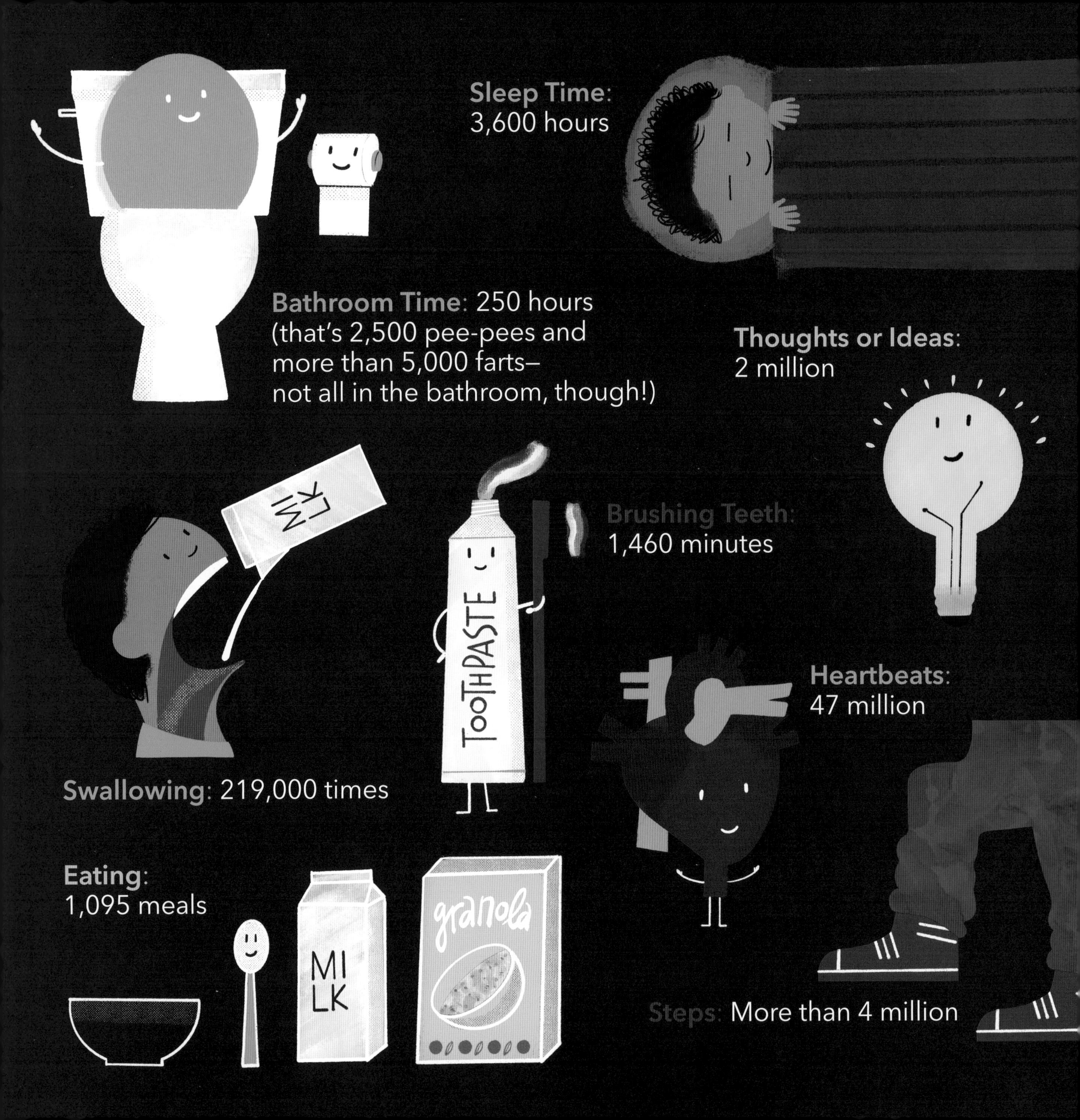

Sleep Time:
3,600 hours

Bathroom Time: 250 hours
(that's 2,500 pee-pees and
more than 5,000 farts—
not all in the bathroom, though!)

Thoughts or Ideas:
2 million

Brushing Teeth:
1,460 minutes

TOOTHPASTE

Heartbeats:
47 million

Swallowing: 219,000 times

Eating:
1,095 meals

MI
LK

granola

Steps: More than 4 million

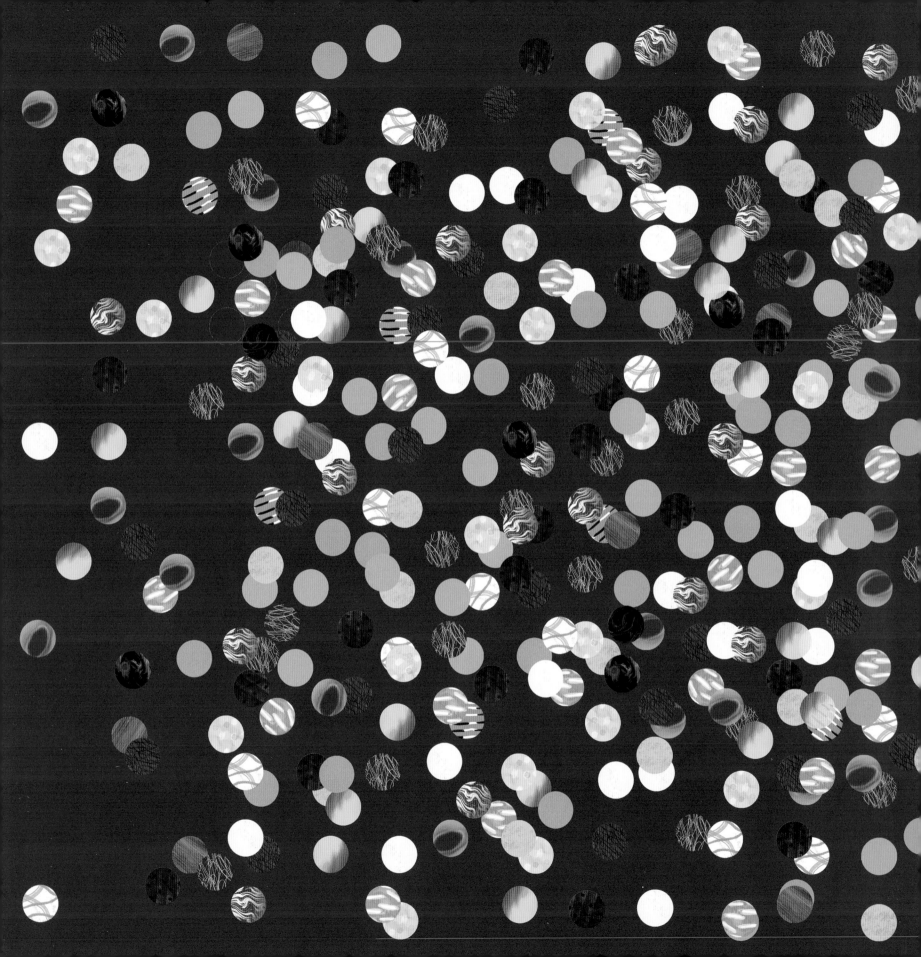